Reflections And Revelations

Lydia Thomas

Presentation by *BookLeaf Publishing*

Web: www.bookleafpub.com

E-mail: info@bookleafpub.com

ISBN: 9789358316957

First edition 2024

To the people who have made my life worth living.

She Is Me

Distinguishing the voices
between the noises,
is the hardest part of all.
Because in the darkest part
of the night's coldest heart,
that's when she'll hear them call.
It's a cold whisper
from a hollow figure
not a shout, scream or cry.
And if she could,
oh, then she would,
she would let it die.

There is no better,
then a world with no 'never'
where she can stay free.
And for this bedtime
and for some time,
I'll forget that she is me.

Just One Bloodstain

Doesn't matter when, doesn't matter where,
doesn't matter why, but it's easy how.
Take that cold blade, place it just there,
it's not rocket science, just do it now!

It might look like self-pity,
attention,
or I'm screaming for some Goddamn aid.
But, could I actually be an exception?
Of course not! I'm like you: afraid!

I've thought for too long on how to go.
My mind wanders when my body stalls,
I try to go quickly and not this slow,
so my courage slips, and the knife falls.

Of course, I'll say it's all their fault,
of course, I'll put the blame on them.
Without their words, I may have support.
Without their names, I would feel again

It is scary,
  It is terrifying.
To be within the tunnel and see no light.
Seeing that darkness is somehow clarifying,

Feeling that steel is somehow right.

I've given up believing in people,
I've cast aside the burden of pain,
With a simple act I can truly be free
The price is just one bloodstain.

Four Seasons

Spring air.
Whispers of life awaken, first breath begins
melodies of birds fill the sky,
petals unfurl, and colours fly.

Summer's embrace.
Scorching sun, green grass beneath our feet.
Laughter echoes, ice cream's first bite,
days stretch, and dreams take flight.

Autumn leaves.
Here comes nature's artwork, hues ablaze,
crisp air dances, a symphony of change,
whispers of farewell, beauty in decay.

Winter breeze.
Ice-cold kisses upon red, rosy cheeks,
snowflakes twirling, a magical tease,
cozy fires, and tinsel-covered trees.

Four seasons.
All align in hushed harmony.
A dance of life and change we see
nature's rhythm, forever free.

Reflection

From the corner of my eye,
I see the judgment from afar.
Stone cold, icy blue,
doors closed, walls up.
Why do you just stand there?
Please just let me through!

I've tried so hard to open,
I've tried so hard to look back,
futile, too much,
impossible, no hope.
Just say something to me!
Why am I never enough?

One day, I'll stand up to you.
One day, I must be stronger!
See me? Rejection.
Hear me? No reply.
Of all the people on this earth,
why are you my reflection?

Love Myself

In a world that seeks
to tear us down,
we rise.

Embracing these flaws,
and scars unseen,
let's find beauty.

For we are more
than just the mirror.
We are love.

In every breath,
and every step,
We. Are. Enough.

No longer bound
by other's judgements,
let's set ourselves free.

Despite the doubt,
despite the pain,
let's learn to 'love myself'.

My Once

Time betrayed us, cruel and unkind,
we danced in the realm of what could be.
Leaving our souls searching when confined
but fate had other plans, it seemed.

No promises made, no vows exchanged,
we soared high on wings of desire,
Just a taste of love, so beautifully strange.
Only to burn within the fire.

The memories linger, haunting my mind,
within my being, a whisper remains.
A bittersweet reminder of that love stays behind,
Of the fun we shared and love that wanes.

And now I'm left with fragments,
Of a love that was never meant to last.
But, oh, how I cherish what we had once,
in that fleeting moment, so beautifully fast.

Nan

A monster grew within an angel.
It devoured her, inch by bloody inch;
from the outside, she was there,
but the light that glowed in her eyes
no longer shone so bright.

The lady who made us corned beef sandwiches,
gave us the coziest of hugs, and bought me
my favourite teddy, which still smells of you.
Her smiles and laughs began to retreat.
The woman I loved, to the moon and back,
began to leave us behind
She was caught in her rocket ship
And we were stuck on Earth.

I never got to say goodbye.
I never got to hold you one last time.
I'm so sorry I never told you I loved you,
But now you free to fly up there,
to fly among the galaxies,
And to out outshine those dull, ol' stars.
I'll look for you, tonight.

Family To The Rescue

In times of great darkness, when shadows loom,
and life's harsh winds begin to consume,
there's a beacon of hope that's always true -
family to the rescue, to pull me through.

Through laughter and tears, they stand by my
side,
with unwavering love, they never hide.
A safety net woven with threads so strong,
family to the rescue, where I know I belong.

Their arms embrace, a shelter from the storm,
A refuge where I'm safe, where I am warm,
Each heartbeat echoes, a symphony of care,
Family to the rescue, they're always there.

Through trials and triumphs, highs and lows,
They lift me up, they help me grow,
With open hearts, they mend my soul,
Family to the rescue, making me whole.

Their love is a lifeline, sturdy and true,
When life's battles rage, they help push through,
Together we weather life's wavy sea,
Family to the rescue, setting me free.

??All the Giggles???

Laughter, like a warm summer breeze,
unleashes joy upon the world.
Spilling from hearts, a contagious disease,
infecting souls, young and old.

It dances like raindrops on a window pane,
melting away troubles and strife.
A soothing balm, it eases pain,
bringing relief to the darkest parts of life.

It echoes through valleys, bouncing off walls,
creating a symphony of glee.
A language universal, understood by all,
uniting humanity, setting us free.

It tickles our spirits, like a playful sprite,
unleashing smiles from deep within.
A moment of respite, a pure delight,
a reminder that life is not all grim.

Oh, laughter, you are a gift divine,
a fleeting moment of pure bliss.
In your embrace, we find the sublime,
a taste of heaven, in a world amiss.

Never Be The Same Tomorrow

The leaves

       f

           a

                l

                    l

                                   from

parents' grip,

                         caressed by

wind's gentle kiss.
 Landing upon

         shards of grass,
they bask in sun's softening glow.

 Withering and w i t h e r i n g,
they decay there

     as summer has now passed on;
 grass trodden to brown, sky rained to grey,
   faces

      deflated
to an ever-present blue.

But the birds left to sing still do

no
echo...
to be found.
And the roses poke their
                 b l o o m s through
never giving up.

Even the windows reflect

                    and capture what is left

          of the world that will never be the same
tomorrow.

My Time Keeper

Every hour was a second with you,
a fleeting moment, a whisper in time,
as the world spun around us,
we danced on the edge of eternity.

In your eyes, I found endless galaxies,
each blink, a universe of mysteries.
And as the seconds melted away,
our souls intertwined in cosmic harmony.

With each passing moment,
Our hearts beat in synchrony.
A rhythm only we could hear,
a melody of love, laughter, and glee.

Every hour was a second with you,
but it truly felt like a lifetime.
For in your presence, time stood still,
and the world ceased its relentless chime.

We painted our days with laughter,
and etched memories in the sands of time.
Every second an eternity of bliss,
in this timeless realm, you were mine.

But alas, the clock's hands kept moving,
and the world demanded its due.
Our hours turned into minutes,
and our seconds vanished from view.

Every hour was a second with you,
a glimpse of heaven, a taste of the divine.
And though time may have stolen you away,
in my heart, you will forever shine.

Fake Love

You speak of deception,
with words so sweet and kind,
but behind those empty promises,
there's a treacherous mind.

Your touch was like fire,
but now I know your façade,
a masquerade of affection
leaving us burned and scared.

You play with emotions,
like the puppeteer on a stage,
pulling heartstrings and creating
a never-ending rage.

But I see through your charade,
I'll be fooled no more.
For in the depths of your deceit
I find strength once more.

So go on with your games,
your lies will no longer sway.
I've learned to see through your disguise.
And now I break away.

The Essence Of Me

A kaleidoscope of shifting hues,
I am an ever-changing tide.
One moment, I'm a thunderous storm,
the next, a gentle breeze.
Is it the pull of the moon,
or others that change my course?
I am a body of contradictions,
a wandering soul in constant flux.

I transform like the seasons,
from vibrant spring to icy winter.
But beneath these shifting layers,
I remain the same at my core.

There is a fire within me,
a spirit that cannot be contained.
I am a vessel of endless possibilities,
ever changing, yet never taken.
So, I embrace this dance of change,
for it is what makes me whole.
In every transformation, I find strength,
and in every shift, a chance to grow.

I don't know why I change so drastically,
but perhaps, it is simply the essence of me.

A boundless, ever-changing spirit,
unfolding with each breath I take.

Chaotic Symphony

In the depths of this mind, chaos resides,
a storm of thoughts, a flood of tides.
Unrestrained, wild, there's no clear design,
the disorderly dance of the muddled mind.

Ideas collide, like stars in the night,
sparking explosions, blinding the lights.
All those visions, fleeting and fast,
like fragments of dreams, they flicker and pass.

Shouts filled with doubt, I hear yet again.
A cry for hope, like sun in the rain.
An orchestra of worries, the 'insane' symphony,
playing incessantly with this chaotic cacophony.

In this place, reason is but a phantom,
Lost like the turmoil, a forgotten anthem.
The mind, a vast canvas, painted in confusion,
searching for solace, a calm conclusion.

Yet amidst all this, a spark ignites,
a glimmer of clarity, guiding our night.
In the heart of the storm, a moment of grace,
Chaos can find order, and thoughts can find
place.

Through this mess, creativity is born.
as chaos gives rise to new ideas, freshly torn.
In the jumble of thoughts, brilliance takes flight,
and in the chaos of the mind, genius can fight!

So, embrace the chaos, let it run free,
for within this madness, there's beauty to see.
For it's in the madness, the mind's wild terrain,
That we find ourselves - crazy, flawed and
insane.

Bewitched

Can the eyes reflect the madness within
when the mask is held so tightly in place?
Can we truly see what is so hidden
when she's worked so hard on her poker face?

Laughter, smiles, jokes and wit can only
hide what she chooses to stow away.
After all, it is her angel that tries to protect
but the demon that's lead her astray.

Can she tell the barest of truths
when she's tried hard to conceal in lies?
Can she trust those around her
when she's helpless to see enemies, not allies?

It is not plague or illness, that stains her inside,
nor something that can truly be fixed.
'It is my curse!', she'll repeatedly cry
as she was, is, and for all time, bewitched.

I'm Fine

'I'm fine', I say, with a careful smile,
a mask of composure I've built for a while.
Behind these eyes, a storm brews,
an eruption of emotions, a battle I'll lose.

I plaster a smile, like a delicate thread,
hoping no one will notice the tears I shed.
Each day passes by, and I play my part
but beneath the surface, I'm falling apart.

I'm fine, they assume, as I laugh and jest,
but inside, my heartache, it never rests.
The weight on my shoulder, I bear alone,
a burden unseen, a struggle unknown

How can I tell them, they can't know.
How do I know if they're friend or foe?
I'm fine, they believe, as I carry on,
yet inside I'm breaking, my spirit withdrawn.

I long for solace, for a moment's release,
to flee these chains, a sense of peace.
It's habit to repeat 'I'm fine' again,
I wish I could believe it now and then.

For in this world, it's easier to pretend
than to unravel my thoughts and think of the end
So I need to wear this mask, though it may
deceive
and hope that someday, I'll truly believe.

Until that day arrives, the secret is mine.
But, it's okay, don't worry, 'I'm fine'.

Revelations and standing ovations

Revelations and standing ovations,
a dance of truth upon life's stage.
Unveiling secrets, untold stories,
in this theatre of endless age.

The curtain rises, anticipation swells,
eager eyes seek wisdom's embrace.
Each revelation, a sacred gift,
unfolding mysteries with grace.

The audience holds their breath,
truths are whispered in hallowed tones.
The symphony of revelations
are resonating under skin and bones.

Standing ovations, thunderous applause,
for the bravery of those who dared
to fight for their just cause
and courageously lay their souls bare.

So let us bask in the revelations
that stir our hearts and move our souls.
For in these moments of divine connection,
We find the essence of being whole.

Forever Bullet Proof

Bulletproof, they stand so tall,
My supermen, never to let me fall,
Through storms and battles, they've held my hand,
Guiding me with courage, helping me understand.

Their presence, a fortress of support,
A shelter from the chaos, a loving port,
Each one a beacon of strength and light,
Together, a constellation in my darkest night.

Their voices, a symphony of encouragement,
Melodies that heal, melodies that mend,
With every word, they lift me higher,
Igniting passion, setting my soul on fire.

In their lyrics, I find solace and peace,
A sanctuary where anxieties cease,
Their love, a balm for my wounded heart,
Mending the scars, creating fresh starts.

In their art, they spread a message so clear,
To embrace oneself, to conquer fear.
To face the world, break every chain

To love yourself, to fight the pain.

My sanctuary, my lifeline, my chosen few,
I'm eternally grateful for all that you do,
In this universe, we shine together,
Stronger, bolder, forever and ever.

Whisper secrets of self-love,
Reminding me of my worth,
In this universe, my own heaven,
With my supermen, forever seven.

Last Domino

26

I   Here, hidden in my mind, are my dominoes.
I   Fragile to life's unstable momentum,
I   stacked in an unstable row

I   A hurtful word to crack my broken wall.
I   A snide comment, a cackle and wail.
I   There, one begins to fall / / /

/   My past is filled with your taunts and scorn.
/   I never fought back, never stood up!
/   Looking back, I mourned.

//   My mind is a disorder playground. /
//   My mind's horrid curses playing daily, /
//   never calming down / / /

/ I   However hard they throw their sticks and stones,
I   I have grown, I will not backdown!
I   I will not reach my last domino! I I I I

www.ingramcontent.com/pod-product-compliance
Lightning Source LLC
LaVergne TN
LVHW021352200726

843509LV00014B/2803